Weather Watchers

Sunshine

Cassie Mayer

Heinemann LIBRARY

H **www.heinemann.co.uk/library**
Visit our website to find out more information about **Heinemann Library** books.

To order:
☎ Phone 44 (0) 1865 888066
🖷 Send a fax to 44 (0) 1865 314091
🖳 Visit the Heinemann Bookshop at www.heinemann.co.uk/library to browse our catalogue and order online.

First published in Great Britain by Heinemann Library,
Halley Court, Jordan Hill, Oxford OX2 8EJ, part of
Harcourt Education. Heinemann is a registered trademark
of Harcourt Education Ltd.

Editorial: Tracey Crawford, Cassie Mayer, Dan Nunn,
and Sarah Chappelow
Design: Jo Hinton-Malivoire
Picture Research: Tracy Cummins, Tracey Engel,
and Ruth Blair
Production: Duncan Gilbert

Originated by Chroma Graphics (Overseas) Pte. Ltd
Printed and bound in China by South China
Printing Company

10 digit ISBN 0 431 18259 0
13 digit ISBN 978 0 431 18259 9

11 10 09 08 07
10 9 8 7 6 5 4 3 2 1

British Library Cataloguing in Publication Data
Mayer, Cassie
  Sunshine. - (Weather watchers)
  1.Sunshine - Juvenile literature
  I.Title
  551.5'271
A full catalogue record for this book is available from the
British Library.

Acknowledgements
The publishers would like to thank the following for
permission to reproduce photographs: Corbis pp. **4**
(cloud; rain, Anthony Redpath), **5** (G. Schuster/zefa), **7**
(Royalty Free), **8** (Theo Allofs), **9** (zefa/Sergio Pitamitz),
10 (Chris Sattlberger), **11** (Royalty Free), **12** (Royalty
Free), **13** (Galen Rowell), **14** (Reuters), **15** (epa/Karl-Josef
Hildenbrand), **16** (Richard Klune), **17** (zefa/S. Andreas),
18 (Royalty Free), **19** (zefa/Jason Horowitz), **20** (George
D. Lepp), **21** (ROB & SAS), **23** (heat wave, Reuters;
snow scene, epa/Karl-Josef Hildenbrand); Getty Images
pp. **4** (lightning; snow, Marc Wilson Photography), **6**
(Tim McGuire).

Cover photograph reproduced with permission of Corbis
(Howard Kingsnorth/zefa). Back cover photograph
reproduced with permission of Corbis (George D. Lepp).

Every effort has been made to contact copyright holders
of any material reproduced in this book. Any omissions
will be rectified in subsequent printings if notice is given
to the publishers.

Contents

What is weather?

There are many types of weather.
Weather changes all the time.

A sunny day is a type of weather.

What is sunshine?

Sunshine is light from the sun.

Sunshine feels warm
on your skin.

Sunshine heats the land.

Sunshine heats the ocean.

The Sun rises in the morning.
Then it is light outside.

The Sun sets in the evening.
Then it is dark outside.

In the middle of the day the Sun is high in the sky. The sunshine is strong.

In the mornings and evenings the Sun is low in the sky. The sunshine is weak.

Sunshine and the seasons

Sunshine is strong in the summer.
Summer days can be hot.

Sunshine is weak in the winter.
Winter days can be cold.

Sunshine around the world

Countries near the equator have strong sunshine. These countries are warm all year.

Countries far from the equator
have weak sunshine. These
countries are cold all year.

Sunshine safety

Sunshine can burn your skin.
Always stay covered in the Sun.

Sunshine can hurt your eyes.
Never look right at the Sun.

How does sunshine help us?

Living things need sunshine to grow.

Sunny days can be fun!

What to wear in the sun

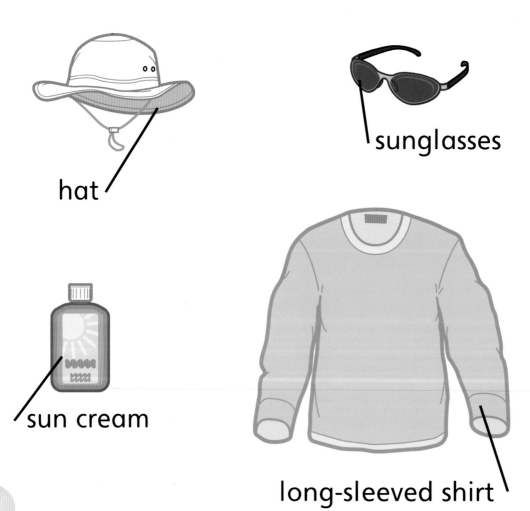

hat

sunglasses

sun cream

long-sleeved shirt

Picture glossary

summer the time of year when it is warmest

winter the time of year when it is coldest

Index

Notes to parents and teachers
Before reading
Talk about different weather. Ask the children which type of weather they like best.
Talk about how the Sun is warmer in the summer than in the winter, as the Sun is closer
in the summer.

After reading
Play "Sun and Rain". Select one child to be the rain and another to be the sun. The rest of
the children run around within a specified area. If caught by the rain, children must stand
still, arms and legs outstretched, until "released" by the Sun who crawls through their legs.
Sing: "The Sun has got his hat on, Hip, Hip, Hip Hurray".
Share with the children the traditional story "The Sun and the Wind".
Sprinkle some mustard seeds on damp newspaper. Place some in a dark cupboard
and the rest on a sunny windowsill. Compare how each grows. Talk about how plants
need sunshine to grow.

Titles in the *Weather Watchers* series include:

Hardback 0 431 18258 2

Hardback 0 431 18256 6

Hardback 0 431 18257 4

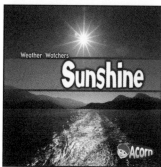

Hardback 0 431 18259 0

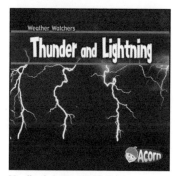

Hardback 0 431 18255 8

Hardback 0 431 18260 4

Find out about other titles from Heinemann Library on our website www.heinemann.co.uk/library